To

_____

From

_____

Broadstreet Publishing™
Racine, WI 53403
Broadstreetpublishing.com

Bible Promises for Women
© 2014 by Broadstreet Publishing

ISBN 978-1-4245-4916-0

Compiled by Michelle Winger
Cover design by Josh Lewandowski
Interior design by James Baker | www.jamesbakerdesign.com

Printed in the United States of America

BIBLE PROMISES
for Women

BroadStreet
PUBLISHING

Contents

Alpha

"I am the Alpha and the Omega, the Beginning and
the End," says the Lord, "who is and who was and
who is to come, the Almighty."

REVELATION 1:8 NKJV

Jesus Christ is the same yesterday and today and forever.

HEBREWS 13:8 NASB

My God will supply all your needs according to
His riches in glory in Christ Jesus.

PHILIPPIANS 4:19 NASB

I fall to my knees and pray to the Father, the Creator of everything in heaven and on earth. I pray that from his glorious, unlimited resources he will empower you with inner strength through his Spirit. Then Christ will make his home in your hearts as you trust in him.

EPHESIANS 3:14–17 NLT

God is the one who provides seed for the farmer and then bread to eat. In the same way, he will provide and increase your resources and then produce a great harvest of generosity in you.

2 CORINTHIANS 9:10 NLT

Abandonment

The LORD himself goes before you and will be with you;
he will never leave you nor forsake you.

DEUTERONOMY 31:8 NIV

God makes a home for the lonely;
He leads out the prisoners into prosperity.

PSALM 68:6 NASB

Those who know your name trust in you,
for you, O LORD, do not abandon
those who search for you.

PSALM 9:10 NLT

GOD made my life complete
when I placed all the pieces before him....
GOD rewrote the text of my life
when I opened the book of my heart to his eyes.

PSALM 18:20, 24 MSG

I will bring the blind by a way they did not know;
I will lead them in paths they have not known.
I will make darkness light before them,
And crooked places straight.
These things will I do for them,
And not forsake them.

ISAIAH 42:16 NKJV

The LORD will not abandon His people
on account of His great name,
because the LORD has been pleased
to make you a people for Himself.

1 SAMUEL 12:22 NASB

I will not abandon you as orphans—I will come to you.

JOHN 14:18 NLT

Abuse

The LORD is near to the brokenhearted
and saves the crushed in spirit.

PSALM 34:18 ESV

LORD, you know the hopes of the helpless.
Surely you will hear their cries and comfort them.
You will bring justice to the orphans and the oppressed,
so mere people can no longer terrify them.

PSALM 10:17–18 NLT

The LORD hears his people
when they call to him for help.
He rescues them from all their troubles.

PSALM 34:17 NLT

You, God, see the trouble of the afflicted;
you consider their grief and take it in hand.
The victims commit themselves to you;
you are the helper of the fatherless.

Psalm 10:14 NIV

So we're not giving up. How could we! Even though
on the outside it often looks like things are falling apart
on us, on the inside, where God is making new life,
not a day goes by without his unfolding grace.

2 Corinthians 4:16 MSG

You, O Lord, are a shield about me,
My glory, and the One who lifts my head.

Psalm 3:3 NASB

Acceptance

I've redeemed you.
I've called your name. You're mine.
When you're in over your head, I'll be there with you.
When you're in rough waters, you will not go down.
When you're between a rock and a hard place,
it won't be a dead end—
Because I am GOD, your personal God,
The Holy of Israel, your Savior.
I paid a huge price for you...!
That's how much you mean to me!
That's how much I love you!

ISAIAH 43:1–4 MSG

If God is for us, who can be against us?

ROMANS 8:31 ESV

The Father gives me the people who are mine. Every one of them will come to me, and I will always accept them.

JOHN 6:37 NCV

Here I am! I stand at the door and knock. If anyone hears my voice and opens the door, I will come in and eat with that person, and they with me.

REVELATION 3:20 NIV

Before he made the world, God chose us to be his very own through what Christ would do for us; he decided then to make us holy in his eyes, without a single fault—we who stand before him covered with his love.

EPHESIANS 1:4 TLB

Addiction

No temptation has overtaken you except what is
common to mankind. And God is faithful; he will not
let you be tempted beyond what you can bear.
But when you are tempted, he will also provide
a way out so that you can endure it.

1 CORINTHIANS 10:13 NIV

Abstain from the passions of the flesh,
which wage war against your soul.

1 PETER 2:11 ESV

Dear brothers and sisters, I plead with you to give your
bodies to God because of all he has done for you.
Let them be a living and holy sacrifice—the kind he will
find acceptable. This is truly the way to worship him.

ROMANS 12:1 NLT

It was for freedom that Christ set us free;
therefore keep standing firm and do not be
subject again to a yoke of slavery.

GALATIANS 5:1 NASB

Anyone who belongs to Christ has become a new person.
The old life is gone; a new life has begun!

2 CORINTHIANS 5:17 NLT

Submit to God. Resist the devil
and he will flee from you.

JAMES 4:7 NKJV

If the Son sets you free, you will be free indeed.

JOHN 8:36 NIV

Anger

Everyone should be quick to listen, slow to speak and slow to become angry, because human anger does not produce the righteousness that God desires.

JAMES 1:19–20 NIV

Brothers and sisters, whatever is true, whatever is noble, whatever is right, whatever is pure, whatever is lovely, whatever is admirable—if anything is excellent or praiseworthy—think about such things.

PHILIPPIANS 4:8 NIV

Whoever is slow to anger has great understanding.

PROVERBS 14:29 ESV

Don't let evil get the best of you;
get the best of evil by doing good.

ROMANS 12:21 MSG

A fool vents all his feelings,
But a wise man holds them back.

PROVERBS 29:11 NKJV

In your anger do not sin: Do not let the sun go down while
you are still angry, and do not give the devil a foothold.

EPHESIANS 4:26–27 NIV

Be not quick in your spirit to become angry,
for anger lodges in the heart of fools.

ECCLESIASTES 7:9 ESV

Sensible people control their temper;
they earn respect by overlooking wrongs.

PROVERBS 19:11 NLT

Anxiety

Cast all your anxiety on him because he cares for you.

1 PETER 5:7 NIV

Do not be anxious about anything, but in every situation,
by prayer and petition, with thanksgiving, present your
requests to God.

PHILIPPIANS 4:6 NIV

I've told you all this so that trusting me, you will be
unshakable and assured, deeply at peace. In this godless
world you will continue to experience difficulties.
But take heart! I've conquered the world.

JOHN 16:33 MSG

In my trouble I cried to the LORD,
And He answered me.

PSALM 120:1 NASB

Let not your heart be troubled.
You are trusting God, now trust in me.

JOHN 14:1 TLB

Say to those with fearful hearts,
"Be strong, and do not fear,
for your God…is coming to save you."

ISAIAH 35:4 NLT

If you make the LORD your refuge,
if you make the Most High your shelter,
no evil will conquer you;
no plague will come near your home.
For he will order his angels
to protect you wherever you go.

PSALM 91:9–11 NLT

Beauty

Don't be concerned about the outward beauty of
fancy hairstyles, expensive jewelry, or beautiful clothes.
You should clothe yourselves instead with the beauty that
comes from within, the unfading beauty of a gentle and
quiet spirit, which is so precious to God.

1 PETER 3:3–4 NLT

I will praise You,
for I am fearfully and wonderfully made;
marvelous are Your works,
and that my soul knows very well.

PSALM 139:14 NKJV

Has anyone by fussing in front of the mirror ever
gotten taller by so much as an inch? All this time
and money wasted on fashion—do you think it makes
that much difference? Instead of looking at the fashions,
walk out into the fields and look at the wildflowers.
They never primp or shop, but have you ever seen color
and design quite like it? The ten best-dressed men and
women in the country look shabby alongside them.

MATTHEW 6:27–29 MSG

The LORD doesn't see things the way you see them.
People judge by outward appearance,
but the LORD looks at the heart.

1 SAMUEL 16:7 NLT

Blessings

Blessed be the God and Father of our Lord Jesus Christ,
who has blessed us in Christ with every spiritual blessing
in the heavenly places, even as he chose us in him
before the foundation of the world, that we should be holy
and blameless before him.

EPHESIANS 1:3–4 ESV

You prepare a feast for me
in the presence of my enemies.
You honor me by anointing my head with oil.
My cup overflows with blessings.

PSALM 23:5 NLT

Taste and see that the LORD is good;
blessed is the one who takes refuge in him!

PSALM 34:8 NIV

The LORD bless you, and keep you;
The LORD make His face shine on you,
And be gracious to you;
The LORD lift up His countenance on you,
And give you peace.

NUMBERS 6:24–26 NASB

How blessed all those in whom you live,
whose lives become roads you travel;
They wind through lonesome valleys, come upon brooks,
discover cool springs and pools brimming with rain!

PSALM 84:5–6 MSG

From his abundance we have all received one
gracious blessing after another.

JOHN 1:16 NLT

Caring

Bear one another's burdens, and so
fulfill the law of Christ.

GALATIANS 6:2 ESV

If anyone has material possessions and sees a brother or
sister in need but has no pity on them, how can the love of
God be in that person? Dear children, let us not love with
words or speech but with actions and in truth.

1 JOHN 3:17–18 NIV

Do not merely look out for your own personal interests, but
also for the interests of others.

PHILIPPIANS 2:4 NASB

I was hungry and you gave me something to eat,

I was thirsty and you gave me something to drink,

I was a stranger and you invited me in, I needed clothes

and you clothed me, I was sick and you looked after me,

I was in prison and you came to visit me....

Whatever you did for one of the least of these brothers

and sisters of mine, you did for me.

MATTHEW 25:35–36, 40 NIV

Pure and genuine religion in the sight of God the Father

means caring for orphans and widows in their distress.

JAMES 1:27 NLT

Compassion

Where is another God like you, who pardons the sins
of the survivors among his people? You cannot
stay angry with your people, for you love to be merciful.
Once again you will have compassion on us. You will tread
our sins beneath your feet; you will throw them into
the depths of the ocean! You will bless us as you
promised Jacob long ago. You will set your love upon us,
as you promised our father Abraham!

MICAH 7:18–20 TLB

Be gracious to me, O God,
according to Your lovingkindness;
According to the greatness of Your compassion
blot out my transgressions.

PSALM 51:1 NASB

You, O Lord, are a God full of compassion, and gracious,
Longsuffering and abundant in mercy and truth.

PSALM 86:15 NKJV

The LORD longs to be gracious to you;
therefore he will rise up to show you compassion.
For the LORD is a God of justice.
Blessed are all who wait for him!

ISAIAH 30:18 NIV

Praise be to the God and Father of our Lord Jesus Christ,
the Father of compassion and the God of all comfort.

2 CORINTHIANS 1:3 NIV

Confidence

Be my rock of refuge,
to which I can always go;
give the command to save me,
for you are my rock and my fortress....
You have been my hope, Sovereign LORD,
my confidence since my youth.

PSALM 71:3, 5 NIV

We can confidently say, "The Lord is my helper;
I will not fear; what can man do to me?"

HEBREWS 13:6 ESV

I am confident of this very thing, that He
who began a good work in you will perfect it
until the day of Christ Jesus.

PHILIPPIANS 1:6 NASB

I can do everything through Christ,
who gives me strength.

PHILIPPIANS 4:13 NLT

Let us then approach God's throne of grace
with confidence, so that we may receive mercy and find
grace to help us in our time of need.

HEBREWS 4:16 NIV

This is the confidence that we have toward him,
that if we ask anything according to his will he hears us.
And if we know that he hears us in whatever we ask,
we know that we have the requests
that we have asked of him.

1 JOHN 5:14–15 ESV

Courage

Be strong and courageous. Do not be frightened,
and do not be dismayed, for the LORD your God
is with you wherever you go.

JOSHUA 1:9 ESV

Love the LORD, all you godly ones!
For the LORD protects those who are loyal to him,
but he harshly punishes the arrogant.
So be strong and courageous,
all you who put your hope in the LORD!

PSALM 31:23–24 NLT

Be strong in the Lord and in his mighty power.
Put on the full armor of God, so that you can
take your stand against the devil's schemes.

EPHESIANS 6:10–11 NIV

Even though I walk through the valley
of the shadow of death,
I fear no evil, for You are with me;
Your rod and Your staff, they comfort me.

PSALM 23:4 NASB

When I am afraid, I put my trust in you.
In God, whose word I praise—
in God I trust and am not afraid.

PSALM 56:3–4 NIV

Be on guard. Stand firm in the faith. Be courageous.
Be strong. And do everything with love.

1 CORINTHIANS 16:13–14 NLT

Courtesy

Seek to do good to one another and to everyone.

1 THESSALONIANS 5:15 ESV

We who are strong must be considerate of those
who are sensitive about things.... We must not just please
ourselves. We should help others do what is right and build
them up in the Lord. For even Christ
didn't live to please himself.

ROMANS 15:1–3 NLT

Do a favor and win a friend forever;
nothing can untie that bond.
Words satisfy the mind as much as fruit does the stomach;
good talk is as gratifying as a good harvest.
Words kill, words give life;
they're either poison or fruit—you choose.

PROVERBS 18:19–21 MSG

Let your speech always be with grace, as though
seasoned with salt, so that you will know
how you should respond to each person.

Colossians 4:6 nasb

Do not forget to show hospitality to strangers,
for by so doing some people have shown hospitality
to angels without knowing it.

Hebrews 13:2 niv

Remind them...to be obedient, to be ready
for every good work, to speak evil of no one,
to avoid quarreling, to be gentle, and to show
perfect courtesy toward all people.

Titus 3:1–2 esv

Depression

Whatever is true, whatever is noble,
whatever is right, whatever is pure, whatever is lovely,
whatever is admirable—if anything is excellent
or praiseworthy—think about such things.

PHILIPPIANS 4:8 NIV

The LORD hears his people
when they call to him for help.
He rescues them from all their troubles.

PSALM 34:17 NLT

He has delivered us from the power of darkness and
conveyed us into the kingdom of the Son of His love.

COLOSSIANS 1:13 NKJV

Why, my soul, are you downcast?
Why so disturbed within me?
Put your hope in God,
for I will yet praise him,
my Savior and my God.

PSALM 42:11 NIV

You, O LORD, are a shield about me,
my glory, and the lifter of my head.

PSALM 3:3 ESV

You are a chosen people, a royal priesthood,
a holy nation, God's special possession, that you may
declare the praises of him who called you out of darkness
into his wonderful light.

1 PETER 2:9 NIV

Encouragement

Let everything you say be good and helpful,
so that your words will be an encouragement
to those who hear them.

EPHESIANS 4:29 NLT

Therefore we do not lose heart, but though our
outer man is decaying, yet our inner man is being renewed
day by day. For momentary, light affliction is producing
for us an eternal weight of glory far beyond all comparison.

2 CORINTHIANS 4:16–17 NASB

The humble will see their God at work and be glad.
Let all who seek God's help be encouraged.

PSALM 69:32 NLT

We ask God to give you complete knowledge of his will and
to give you spiritual wisdom and understanding.
Then the way you live will always honor and
please the Lord, and your lives will produce
every kind of good fruit. All the while, you will grow
as you learn to know God better and better.

COLOSSIANS 1:9–10 NLT

Let us consider how to stir up one another to love
and good works not neglecting to meet together,
as is the habit of some, but encouraging one another.

HEBREWS 10:24–25 ESV

Enthusiasm

Whatever you do, work heartily, as for the Lord and
not for men, knowing that from the Lord you
will receive the inheritance as your reward.
You are serving the Lord Christ.

COLOSSIANS 3:23–24 ESV

When I discovered your words, I devoured them.
They are my joy and my heart's delight, for I
bear your name, O LORD God of Heaven's Armies.

JEREMIAH 15:16 NLT

Make the most of every opportunity.
Let your conversation be always full of grace.

COLOSSIANS 4:5–6 NIV

You will light my lamp;
The LORD my God will enlighten my darkness.
For by You I can run against a troop,
By my God I can leap over a wall.

PSALM 18:28–29 NKJV

Oh, how sweet the light of day,
and how wonderful to live in the sunshine!
Even if you live a long time,
don't take a single day for granted.
Take delight in each light-filled hour.

ECCLESIASTES 11:7–8 MSG

Eternity

Before the mountains were brought forth,
or ever you had formed the earth and the world,
from everlasting to everlasting you are God.

PSALM 90:2 ESV

We are citizens of heaven, where the Lord
Jesus Christ lives. And we are eagerly waiting for him to
return as our Savior. He will take our weak mortal bodies
and change them into glorious bodies like his own,
using the same power with which he
will bring everything under his control.

PHILIPPIANS 3:20–21 NLT

I will come back and take you to be with me
that you also may be where I am.

JOHN 14:3 NIV

Surely goodness and mercy shall follow me
All the days of my life;
And I will dwell in the house of the Lord
Forever.

Psalm 23:6 nkjv

We fix our eyes not on what is seen,
but on what is unseen. For what is seen is temporary,
but what is unseen is eternal.

2 Corinthians 4:18 niv

I'm asking God for one thing, only one thing:
To live with Him in His house my whole life long.
I'll contemplate His beauty; I'll study at His feet.

Psalm 27:4 msg

Excellence

It is my prayer that your love may abound more and more,
with knowledge and all discernment, so that you
may approve what is excellent, and so be pure
and blameless for the day of Christ.

PHILIPPIANS 1:9–10 ESV

His divine power has granted to us everything
pertaining to life and godliness, through the
true knowledge of Him who called us by His own
glory and excellence.

2 PETER 1:3 NASB

Whether you eat or drink, or whatever you do,
do all to the glory of God.

1 CORINTHIANS 10:31 NKJV

Do your best to present yourself to God as one approved,
a worker who does not need to be ashamed and
who correctly handles the word of truth.

2 Timothy 2:15 niv

Many women have done excellently,
but you surpass them all.
Charm is deceitful, and beauty is vain,
but a woman who fears the Lord is to be praised.
Give her of the fruit of her hands,
and let her works praise her in the gates.

Proverbs 31:29–31 esv

Faith

Faith is confidence in what we hope for and assurance about what we do not see.

HEBREWS 11:1 NIV

Through Christ you have come to trust in God. And you have placed your faith and hope in God because he raised Christ from the dead and gave him great glory.

1 PETER 1:21 NLT

Without faith it is impossible to please God, because anyone who comes to him must believe that he exists and that he rewards those who earnestly seek him.

HEBREWS 11:6 NIV

Faith comes by hearing, and hearing by the word of God.

ROMANS 10:17 NKJV

If you have faith like a grain of mustard seed, you will say to this mountain, "Move from here to there," and it will move, and nothing will be impossible for you.

MATTHEW 17:20 ESV

As we pray to our God and Father about you, we think of your faithful work, your loving deeds, and the enduring hope you have because of our Lord Jesus Christ.

1 THESSALONIANS 1:3 NLT

As many as received Him, to them He gave the right to become children of God, even to those who believe in His name.

JOHN 1:12 NASB

Faithfulness

Your lovingkindness, O LORD, extends to the heavens,
Your faithfulness reaches to the skies.

PSALM 36:5 NASB

God is faithful. He will not allow the temptation to be
more than you can stand. When you are tempted, he will
show you a way out so that you can endure.

1 CORINTHIANS 10:13 NLT

LORD, you are my God;
I will exalt you and praise your name,
for in perfect faithfulness
you have done wonderful things,
things planned long ago.

ISAIAH 25:1 NIV

The word of the LORD is upright,
and all his work is done in faithfulness.

PSALM 33:4 ESV

The steadfast love of the LORD never ceases;
his mercies never come to an end;
they are new every morning;
great is your faithfulness.

LAMENTATIONS 3:22–23 ESV

I will sing of the LORD's great love forever;
with my mouth I will make your faithfulness known
through all generations.
I will declare that your love stands firm forever,
that you have established your faithfulness in heaven itself.

PSALM 89:1–2 NIV

Fear

Don't be afraid, for I am with you.
Don't be discouraged, for I am your God.
I will strengthen you and help you.
I will hold you up with my victorious right hand.

ISAIAH 41:10 NLT

The name of the LORD is a strong tower;
The righteous runs into it and is safe.

PROVERBS 18:10 NASB

God is our refuge and strength,
an ever-present help in trouble.

PSALM 46:1 NIV

God has not given us a spirit of fear,
but of power and of love and of a sound mind.

2 TIMOTHY 1:7 NKJV

There is no room in love for fear. Well-formed love
banishes fear. Since fear is crippling, a fearful life—
fear of death, fear of judgment—is one
not yet fully formed in love.

1 John 4:18 msg

The Lord is my light and my salvation;
whom shall I fear?
The Lord is the stronghold of my life;
of whom shall I be afraid?

Psalm 27:1 esv

When you lie down, you will not be afraid;
when you lie down, your sleep will be sweet.

Proverbs 3:24 niv

Finances

My God will meet all your needs according to
the riches of his glory in Christ Jesus.

PHILIPPIANS 4:19 NIV

Whoever wishes to save his life will lose it; but whoever
loses his life for My sake will find it. For what will it profit
a man if he gains the whole world and forfeits his soul?
Or what will a man give in exchange for his soul?

MATTHEW 16:25–26 NASB

Don't love money; be satisfied with what you have.
For God has said, "I will never fail you.
I will never abandon you."

HEBREWS 13:5 NLT

As for the rich in this present age, charge them not
to be haughty, nor to set their hopes on the
uncertainty of riches, but on God, who richly provides us
with everything to enjoy.

1 TIMOTHY 6:17 ESV

With me are riches and honor,
enduring wealth and prosperity.
My fruit is better than fine gold;
what I yield surpasses choice silver.
I walk in the way of righteousness,
along the paths of justice,
bestowing a rich inheritance on those who love me
and making their treasuries full.

PROVERBS 8:18–21 NIV

Flexibility

Blessed the woman, who listens to me,
awake and ready for me each morning,
alert and responsive as I start my day's work.
When you find me, you find life, real life,
to say nothing of GOD's good pleasure.

PROVERBS 8:34–35 MSG

Accept other believers...and don't argue with them about
what they think is right or wrong. For instance...those
who worship the Lord on a special day do it to honor him.
Those who eat any kind of food do so to honor the Lord,
since they give thanks to God before eating. And those who
refuse to eat certain foods also want to please
the Lord and give thanks to God.

ROMANS 14:1–2, 6 NLT

I know what it is to be in need, and I know what it is
to have plenty. I have learned the secret of being
content in any and every situation, whether well fed or
hungry, whether living in plenty or in want.
I can do all this through him who gives me strength.

PHILIPPIANS 4:12–13 NIV

I prefer a flexible heart to an inflexible ritual.

MATTHEW 12:7 MSG

You are our Father;
We are the clay, and You our potter;
And all we are the work of Your hand.

ISAIAH 64:8 NKJV

Forgiveness

If we confess our sins, He is faithful and just to forgive us
our sins and to cleanse us from all unrighteousness.

1 John 1:9 nkjv

If you forgive other people when they sin against you,
your heavenly Father will also forgive you.

Matthew 6:14 niv

He is so rich in kindness and grace that he purchased our
freedom with the blood of his Son and forgave our sins.

Ephesians 1:7 nlt

Her sins—and they are many—have been forgiven,
so she has shown me much love. But a person
who is forgiven little shows only little love.

Luke 7:47 nlt

As far as the east is from the west,
So far has He removed our transgressions from us.

PSALM 103:12 NASB

Whenever you stand praying, forgive,
if you have anything against anyone, so that your Father
also who is in heaven may forgive you.

MARK 11:25 ESV

My sacrifice, O God, is a broken spirit;
a broken and contrite heart you, God, will not despise.

PSALM 51:17 NIV

For You, Lord, are good, and ready to forgive,
And abundant in mercy to all those who call upon You.

PSALM 86:5 NKJV

Friendship

Greater love has no one than this:
to lay down one's life for one's friends.
You are my friends if you do what I command.
I no longer call you servants, because a servant
does not know his master's business. Instead, I have
called you friends, for everything that I learned
from my Father I have made known to you.

JOHN 15:13–15 NIV

There are "friends" who pretend to be friends,
but there is a friend who sticks closer than a brother.

PROVERBS 18:24 TLB

A friend loves at all times.

PROVERBS 17:17 NKJV

Love prospers when a fault is forgiven,
but dwelling on it separates close friends.

PROVERBS 17:9 NLT

The right word at the right time
is like a custom-made piece of jewelry,
And a wise friend's timely reprimand
is like a gold ring slipped on your finger.
Reliable friends who do what they say
are like cool drinks in sweltering heat—refreshing!

PROVERBS 25:12–13 MSG

Do to others whatever you would like them to do to you.
This is the essence of all that is taught
in the law and the prophets.

MATTHEW 7:12 NLT

Generosity

It is more blessed to give than to receive.

ACTS 20:35 NIV

One man gives freely, yet gains even more;
another withholds unduly, but comes to poverty.
A generous man will prosper;
he who refreshes others will himself be refreshed.

PROVERBS 11:24–25 NIV

Let each one give as he purposes in his heart,
not grudgingly or of necessity;
for God loves a cheerful giver.

2 CORINTHIANS 9:7 NKJV

Whoever is generous to the poor lends to the LORD,
and he will repay him for his deed.

PROVERBS 19:17 ESV

When you give to the needy, do not let your left hand know
what your right hand is doing, so that your giving
may be in secret. Then your Father, who sees
what is done in secret, will reward you.

MATTHEW 6:3–4 NIV

You shall generously give to him, and your heart
shall not be grieved when you give to him, because
for this thing the LORD your God will bless you in all your
work and in all your undertakings.

DEUTERONOMY 15:10 NASB

The generous will themselves be blessed,
for they share their food with the poor.

PROVERBS 22:9 NIV

Goodness

Taste and see that the Lord is good;
blessed is the one who takes refuge in him.

PSALM 34:8 NIV

Everything God created is good, and nothing is to be
rejected if it is received with thanksgiving.

1 TIMOTHY 4:4 NIV

The Lord is good to all,
and his mercy is over all that he has made.

PSALM 145:9 ESV

How great is the goodness
you have stored up for those who fear you.
You lavish it on those who come to you for protection,
blessing them before the watching world.

PSALM 31:19 NLT

Work with enthusiasm, as though you were working for the Lord rather than for people. Remember that the Lord will reward each one of us for the good we do.

EPHESIANS 6:7–8 NLT

Examine everything carefully; hold fast to that which is good; abstain from every form of evil.

1 THESSALONIANS 5:22–23 NASB

A good man's speech reveals the rich treasures within him.

MATTHEW 12:35 TLB

Praise the LORD!
Oh, give thanks to the LORD, for He is good!
For His mercy endures forever.

PSALM 106:1 NKJV

Grace

Let us then with confidence draw near
to the throne of grace, that we may receive mercy and
find grace to help in time of need.

HEBREWS 4:16 ESV

God is so rich in mercy, and he loved us so much,
that even though we were dead because of our sins,
he gave us life when he raised Christ from the dead.
(It is only by God's grace that you have been saved!)...
God saved you by his grace when you believed.
And you can't take credit for this; it is a gift from God.
Salvation is not a reward for the good things we
have done, so none of us can boast about it.

EPHESIANS 2:4–5, 8–9 NLT

Sin...doesn't, have a chance in competition with the
aggressive forgiveness we call *grace*. When it's
sin versus grace, grace wins hands down. All sin can do is
threaten us with death.... Grace...invites us into life—
a life that goes on and on and on, world without end.

ROMANS 5:20–21 MSG

He gives more grace. Therefore He says:
"God resists the proud,
But gives grace to the humble."

JAMES 4:6 NKJV

Sin shall no longer be your master, because you
are not under the law, but under grace.

ROMANS 6:14 NIV

Grief

May our Lord Jesus Christ himself and God our Father,
who loved us and by his grace gave us eternal comfort and
a wonderful hope, comfort you and strengthen you.

2 THESSALONIANS 2:16–17 NLT

He turned my sorrow into joy!
He took away my clothes of mourning
and clothed me with joy.

PSALM 30:11 TLB

The ransomed of the LORD will return.
They will enter Zion with singing;
everlasting joy will crown their heads.
Gladness and joy will overtake them,
and sorrow and sighing will flee away.

ISAIAH 35:10 NIV

Blessed be the God...of all comfort, who comforts us in all our tribulation, that we may be able to comfort those who are in any trouble, with the comfort with which we ourselves are comforted by God.

2 Corinthians 1:3–4 nkjv

To all who mourn...he will give: beauty for ashes; joy instead of mourning; praise instead of heaviness. For God has planted them like strong and graceful oaks for his own glory.

Isaiah 61:3 tlb

He will once again fill your mouth with laughter and your lips with shouts of joy.

Job 8:21 nlt

Guidance

Guide me in your truth and teach me,
for you are God my Savior,
and my hope is in you all day long.

PSALM 25:5 NIV

Trust in the LORD with all your heart,
And lean not on your own understanding;
In all your ways acknowledge Him,
And He shall direct your paths.

PROVERBS 3:5–6 NKJV

We can make our plans,
but the LORD determines our steps.

PROVERBS 16:9 NLT

I will instruct you and teach you in the way you should go;
I will counsel you with my loving eye on you.

PSALM 32:8 NIV

The Lord directs the steps of the godly.
He delights in every detail of their lives.
Though they stumble, they will never fall,
for the Lord holds them by the hand.

Psalm 37:23–24 nlt

Whether you turn to the right or to the left,
your ears will hear a voice behind you, saying,
"This is the way; walk in it."

Isaiah 30:21 niv

Listen to advice and accept discipline,
and at the end you will be counted among the wise.

Proverbs 19:20 niv

The true children of God are those
who let God's Spirit lead them.

Romans 8:14 ncv

Health

He was pierced for our transgressions,
he was crushed for our iniquities;
the punishment that brought us peace was on him,
and by his wounds we are healed.

ISAIAH 53:5 NIV

My child, pay attention to what I say.
Listen carefully to my words.
Don't lose sight of them.
Let them penetrate deep into your heart,
for they bring life to those who find them,
and healing to their whole body.

PROVERBS 4:20–22 NLT

Daughter, your faith has made you well; go in peace
and be healed of your affliction.

MARK 5:34 NASB

A cheerful heart does good like medicine.

PROVERBS 17:22 TLB

Trust GOD from the bottom of your heart;
don't try to figure out everything on your own.
Listen for GOD's voice in everything you do,
everywhere you go;
he's the one who will keep you on track.
Don't assume that you know it all.
Run to GOD! Run from evil!
Your body will glow with health,
your very bones will vibrate with life!

PROVERBS 3:5–8 MSG

The world and its desires pass away,
but whoever does the will of God lives forever.

1 JOHN 2:17 NIV

Helpfulness

Carry each other's burdens, and in this way you will
fulfill the law of Christ.... Therefore, as we have
opportunity, let us do good to all people.

GALATIANS 6:2, 10 NIV

Who is the greater, one who reclines at table or one
who serves? Is it not the one who reclines at table?
But I am among you as the one who serves.

LUKE 22:27 ESV

Give generously, for your gifts will return to you later.
Divide your gifts among many, for in the days ahead
you yourself may need much help.

ECCLESIASTES 11:1–2 TLB

Let the message about Christ, in all its richness,
fill your lives. Teach and counsel each other with all
the wisdom he gives. Sing psalms and hymns and
spiritual songs to God with thankful hearts.
And whatever you do or say, do it as a representative of the
Lord Jesus, giving thanks through him to God the Father.

COLOSSIANS 3:16–17 NLT

God has given each of you a gift from his great variety of
spiritual gifts. Use them well to serve one another.

1 PETER 4:10–11 NLT

Even the Son of Man did not come to be served, but to
serve, and to give His life a ransom for many.

MARK 10:45 NKJV

Honesty

Speaking the truth in love, we will grow to become
in every respect the mature body of him
who is the head, that is, Christ.

EPHESIANS 4:15 NIV

Putting away lying, "Let each one of you speak truth with
his neighbor," for we are members of one another.

EPHESIANS 4:25 NKJV

Truthful words stand the test of time,
but lies are soon exposed.

PROVERBS 12:19 NLT

Do not lie to one another, since you laid aside the old self
with its evil practices, and have put on the new self who is
being renewed to a true knowledge.

COLOSSIANS 3:9-10 NASB

Good people who live honest lives
will be a blessing to their children.

Proverbs 20:7 NCV

A good name is to be chosen rather than great riches,
Loving favor rather than silver and gold.

Proverbs 22:1 NKJV

The Lord detests lying lips,
but he delights in people who are trustworthy.

Proverbs 12:22 NIV

The highway of the upright avoids evil;
he who guards his way guards his life.

Proverbs 16:17 NIV

Those who deal truthfully are His delight.

Proverbs 12:22 NKJV

Hope

We can rejoice, too, when we run into problems
and trials, for we know that they help us
develop endurance. And endurance develops strength of
character, and character strengthens our confident
hope of salvation. And this hope will not lead
to disappointment. For we know how dearly God loves us,
because he has given us the Holy Spirit to fill
our hearts with his love.

ROMANS 5:3–5 NLT

Blessed be the God and Father of our Lord Jesus Christ!
According to his great mercy, he has caused us
to be born again to a living hope through the
resurrection of Jesus Christ.

1 PETER 1:3 ESV

May the God of hope fill you with all joy and peace
as you trust in him, so that you may overflow with hope
by the power of the Holy Spirit.

ROMANS 15:13 NIV

GOD...rekindles burned-out lives with fresh hope,
Restoring dignity and respect to their lives—
a place in the sun!

1 SAMUEL 2:7–8 MSG

The LORD is good to those whose hope is in him,
to the one who seeks him.

LAMENTATIONS 3:25 NIV

Humility

In your relationships with one another,
have the same mindset as Christ Jesus:
Who, being in very nature God,
did not consider equality with God
something to be used to his own advantage;
rather, he made himself nothing
by taking the very nature of a servant,
being made in human likeness.
And being found in appearance as a man,
he humbled himself
by becoming obedient to death—
even death on a cross!
Therefore God exalted him to the highest place
and gave him the name that is above every name.

PHILIPPIANS 2:5–9 NIV

Be content with who you are, and don't put on airs.
God's strong hand is on you; he'll promote you
at the right time. Live carefree before God;
he is most careful with you.

1 PETER 5:6–7 MSG

Humble yourselves in the sight of the Lord,
and He will lift you up.

JAMES 4:10 NKJV

The LORD has told you what is good,
and this is what he requires of you:
to do what is right, to love mercy,
and to walk humbly with your God.

MICAH 6:8 NLT

Inspiration

You are the light of the world. A city set on a hill
cannot be hidden. Nor do people light a lamp
and put it under a basket, but on a stand, and it gives light
to all in the house. In the same way, let your light
shine before others, so that they may see your good works
and give glory to your Father who is in heaven.

MATTHEW 5:14–16 ESV

The precepts of the LORD are right,
giving joy to the heart.
The commands of the LORD are radiant,
giving light to the eyes.

PSALM 19:8 NIV

Your laws are my treasure; they are my heart's delight.

PSALM 119:111 NLT

Pursue a righteous life—a life of wonder, faith, love,
steadiness, courtesy. Run hard and fast in the faith.
Seize the eternal life, the life you were called to,
the life you so fervently embraced in the presence
of so many witnesses.

1 TIMOTHY 6:11–12 MSG

I am the Light of the world; he who follows Me will not
walk in the darkness, but will have the Light of life.

JOHN 8:12 NASB

Joy

Be truly glad! There is wonderful joy ahead.... You love him
even though you have never seen him. Though you
do not see him now, you trust him; and you rejoice
with a glorious, inexpressible joy.

1 Peter 1:6, 8 nlt

You will go out in joy
and be led forth in peace;
the mountains and hills
will burst into song before you,
and all the trees of the field
will clap their hands.

Isaiah 55:12 niv

I have told you this so that my joy may be in you
and that your joy may be complete.

John 15:11 niv

Let all those rejoice who put their trust in You;
Let them ever shout for joy, because You defend them;
Let those also who love Your name
Be joyful in You.

PSALM 5:11 NKJV

Until now you have not asked for anything in my name.
Ask and you will receive, and your joy will be complete.

JOHN 16:24 NIV

Our mouth was filled with laughter,
and our tongue with shouts of joy.

PSALM 126:2 ESV

May the God of hope fill you with all joy
and peace in believing.

ROMANS 15:13 NKJV

Justice

He will not judge by appearance, false evidence,
or hearsay, but will defend the poor and the exploited.
He will rule against the wicked who oppress them. For he
will be clothed with fairness and with truth.

ISAIAH 11:3–5 TLB

The LORD secures justice for the poor
and upholds the cause of the needy.

PSALM 140:12 NIV

Righteousness and justice
are the foundation of Your throne.

PSALM 89:14 NKJV

Beloved, do not avenge yourselves, but rather
give place to wrath; for it is written, "Vengeance is Mine,
I will repay," says the Lord.

ROMANS 12:19 NKJV

Seek justice, correct oppression;
bring justice to the fatherless,
plead the widow's cause.

ISAIAH 1:17 ESV

To do what is right and just
is more acceptable to the LORD than sacrifice.

PROVERBS 21:3 NIV

He did not retaliate when he was insulted,
nor threaten revenge when he suffered.
He left his case in the hands of God,
who always judges fairly.

1 PETER 2:23 NLT

Look, I am coming soon! My reward is with me, and I will
give to each person according to what they have done.

REVELATION 22:12 NIV

Kindness

Love your enemies, do good to them, and lend to them
without expecting to get anything back. Then your reward
will be great, and you will be children of the Most High.

LUKE 6:35 NIV

When she speaks, her words are wise,
and she gives instructions with kindness.

PROVERBS 31:26 NLT

If anyone has material possessions and sees a brother or
sister in need but has no pity on them, how can the love of
God be in that person? Dear children, let us not love with
words or speech but with actions and in truth.

1 JOHN 3:17–18 NIV

Be kind and compassionate to one another.

EPHESIANS 4:32 NIV

Do you presume on the riches of his kindness
and forbearance and patience, not knowing that God's
kindness is meant to lead you to repentance?

Romans 2:4 esv

I will tell of the kindnesses of the Lord,
the deeds for which he is to be praised,
according to all the Lord has done for us…
according to his compassion and many kindnesses.

Isaiah 63:7 niv

His merciful kindness is great toward us,
And the truth of the Lord endures forever.
Praise the Lord!

Psalm 117:2 nkjv

Loneliness

The LORD is near to all who call on him,
to all who call on him in truth.

PSALM 145:18 NIV

O LORD, You have searched me and known me.
You know my sitting down and my rising up;
You understand my thought afar off.
You comprehend my path and my lying down,
And are acquainted with all my ways.
For there is not a word on my tongue,
But behold, O LORD, You know it altogether.

PSALM 139:1–4 NKJV

Turn to me and have mercy,
for I am alone and in deep distress.

PSALM 25:16 NLT

I am sure that neither death nor life,
nor angels nor rulers, nor things present
nor things to come, nor powers, nor height
nor depth, nor anything else in all creation,
will be able to separate us from
the love of God in Christ Jesus our Lord.

ROMANS 8:38–39 ESV

By this we know that we abide in Him and He in us,
because He has given us of His Spirit.

1 JOHN 4:13 NASB

Behold, I am with you always, to the end of the age.

MATTHEW 28:20 ESV

Loss

God's dwelling place is now among the people, and
he will dwell with them. They will be his people,
and God himself will be with them and be their God.
He will wipe every tear from their eyes. There will
be no more death or mourning or crying or pain,
for the old order of things has passed away.

REVELATION 21:3–4 NIV

May your unfailing love be my comfort
according to your promise to your servant.

PSALM 119:76 NIV

Those who sow in tears shall reap with shouts of joy!

PSALM 126:5 ESV

Come to me, all you who are weary and burdened,
and I will give you rest. Take my yoke upon you and learn
from me, for I am gentle and humble in heart,
and you will find rest for your souls.

MATTHEW 11:28–29 NIV

Unless the LORD had helped me,
I would soon have settled in the silence of the grave.
I cried out, "I am slipping!"
but your unfailing love, O LORD, supported me.
When doubts filled my mind,
your comfort gave me renewed hope and cheer.

PSALM 94:17–19 NLT

Love

Satisfy us in the morning with your unfailing love,
that we may sing for joy and be glad all our days.

PSALM 90:14 NIV

Three things will last forever—faith, hope, and love—
and the greatest of these is love.

1 CORINTHIANS 13:13 NLT

You, O Lord, are good and forgiving,
abounding in steadfast love to all who call upon you.

PSALM 86:5 ESV

This is how much God loved the world: He gave his Son,
his one and only Son. And this is why: so that no one need
be destroyed; by believing in him, anyone can have
a whole and lasting life.

JOHN 3:16 MSG

Know therefore that the Lord your God is God;
he is the faithful God, keeping his covenant of love
to a thousand generations of those who love him
and keep his commandments.

Deuteronomy 7:9 niv

Let love be without hypocrisy. Abhor what is evil.
Cling to what is good. Be kindly affectionate to one another
with brotherly love.

Romans 12:9–10 nkjv

Let love and faithfulness never leave you;
bind them around your neck,
write them on the tablet of your heart.

Proverbs 3:3 niv

Patience

They who wait for the LORD
shall renew their strength;
they shall mount up with wings like eagles;
they shall run and not be weary;
they shall walk and not faint.

ISAIAH 40:31 ESV

All of you be harmonious, sympathetic, brotherly,
kindhearted, and humble in spirit; not returning evil for
evil or insult for insult, but giving a blessing instead;
for you were called for the very purpose
that you might inherit a blessing.

1 PETER 3:8–9 NASB

Follow the example of those who are going to inherit
God's promises because of their faith and endurance.

HEBREWS 6:12 NLT

Make me truly happy by agreeing wholeheartedly with each other, loving one another, and working together with one mind and purpose.

PHILIPPIANS 2:2 NLT

Be of the same mind toward one another. Do not set your mind on high things, but associate with the humble. Do not be wise in your own opinion.

ROMANS 12:16 NKJV

Rest in the LORD and wait patiently for Him.... Those who wait for the LORD, they will inherit the land.

PSALM 37:7–9 NASB

May the God of endurance and encouragement grant you to live in such harmony with one another.

ROMANS 15:5–7 ESV

Peace

Peace I leave with you; my peace I give you. I do not give to you as the world gives. Do not let your hearts be troubled and do not be afraid.

JOHN 14:27 NIV

These things I have spoken to you, so that in Me you may have peace. In the world you have tribulation, but take courage; I have overcome the world.

JOHN 16:33 NASB

If people's thinking is controlled by the sinful self, there is death. But if their thinking is controlled by the Spirit, there is life and peace.

ROMANS 8:6 NCV

God is not a God of confusion but of peace.

1 CORINTHIANS 14:33 NASB

Let the peace of Christ rule in your hearts, since as members of one body you were called to peace.

COLOSSIANS 3:15 NIV

Those who love your instructions have great peace and do not stumble.

PSALM 119:165 NLT

May the Lord of peace himself give you peace at all times and in every way. The Lord be with all of you.

2 THESSALONIANS 3:16 NIV

The LORD will give strength to His people;
The LORD will bless His people with peace.

PSALM 29:11 NKJV

Perseverance

Consider it pure joy...whenever you face trials
of many kinds, because you know that the testing of your
faith develops perseverance. Perseverance must finish
its work so that you may be mature and complete,
not lacking anything.

JAMES 1:2–4 NIV

God blesses those who patiently endure testing
and temptation. Afterward they will receive the crown of
life that God has promised to those who love him.

JAMES 1:12 NLT

Let us not grow weary of doing good, for in due season
we will reap, if we do not give up.

GALATIANS 6:9 ESV

Since we are surrounded by such a great cloud of witnesses, let us throw off everything that hinders and the sin that so easily entangles. And let us run with perseverance the race marked out for us, fixing our eyes on Jesus, the pioneer and perfecter of faith. For the joy set before him he endured the cross, scorning its shame, and sat down at the right hand of the throne of God. Consider him who endured such opposition from sinners, so that you will not grow weary and lose heart.

HEBREWS 12:1–3 NIV

May the Lord direct your hearts into God's love and Christ's perseverance.

2 THESSALONIANS 3:5 NIV

Praise

Praise the LORD!
Praise God in his sanctuary;
praise him in his mighty heavens!
Praise him for his mighty deeds;
praise him according to his excellent greatness!...
Let everything that has breath praise the LORD!

PSALM 150:1–2, 6 ESV

Let us continually offer the sacrifice of praise to God,
that is, the fruit of our lips, giving thanks to His name.

HEBREWS 13:15 NKJV

O LORD, You are my God.
I will exalt You,
I will praise Your name,
For You have done wonderful things.

ISAIAH 25:1 NKJV

Praise the LORD from the heavens;
praise him in the heights above.
Praise him, all his angels;
praise him, all his heavenly hosts.
Praise him, sun and moon;
praise him, all you shining stars.
Praise him, you highest heavens
and you waters above the skies.
Let them praise the name of the LORD,
for at his command they were created.

PSALM 148:1–5 NIV

Sing to the LORD a new song,
And His praise from the ends of the earth.

ISAIAH 42:10 NKJV

Prayer

Ask and it will be given to you; seek
and you will find; knock and the door will be
opened to you. For everyone who asks receives;
he who seeks finds; and to him who knocks,
the door will be opened.

MATTHEW 7:7–8 NIV

My voice You shall hear in the morning, O LORD;
In the morning I will direct it to You,
And I will look up.

PSALM 5:3 NKJV

Confess your sins to each other and pray for each other so
that you may be healed. The prayer of a righteous person is
powerful and effective.

JAMES 5:16 NIV

Pray about everything. Tell God what you need,
and thank him for all he has done.

PHILIPPIANS 4:6 NLT

The Spirit also helps our weakness; for we do not know
how to pray as we should, but the Spirit Himself intercedes
for us with groanings too deep for words.

ROMANS 8:26 NASB

You, God, are my God, earnestly I seek you;
I thirst for you, my whole being longs for you,
in a dry and parched land where there is no water.

PSALM 63:1 NIV

Pray without ceasing.

1 THESSALONIANS 5:17 NKJV

Promises

Your promises have been thoroughly tested,
and your servant loves them.
My eyes stay open through the watches of the night,
that I may meditate on your promises.

PSALM 119:140, 148 NIV

Not one word of all the good words which the LORD your
God spoke concerning you has failed; all have been fulfilled
for you, not one of them has failed.

JOSHUA 23:14 NASB

To him who is able to do immeasurably more than all
we ask or imagine, according to his power that is at work
within us, to him be glory...for ever and ever! Amen.

EPHESIANS 3:20–21 NIV

The LORD always keeps his promises;
he is gracious in all he does.

PSALM 145:13 NLT

You believe in God, believe also in Me.
In My Father's house are many mansions.... I go to prepare
a place for you. And if I go and prepare a place for you,
I will come again and receive you to Myself;
that where I am, there you may be also.

JOHN 14:1–3 NKJV

All of God's promises have been fulfilled in Christ
with a resounding "Yes!"

2 CORINTHIANS 1:20 NLT

Purpose

Live as citizens of heaven, conducting yourselves in a
manner worthy of the Good News about Christ…
standing together with one spirit and one purpose,
fighting together for the faith. Don't be intimidated in any
way by your enemies. This will be a sign to them that you
are going to be saved, even by God himself.

PHILIPPIANS 1:27–28 NLT

Be attentive to my words;
incline your ear to my sayings.
Let them not escape from your sight;
keep them within your heart.
Let your eyes look directly forward,
and your gaze be straight before you.

PROVERBS 4:20–21, 25 ESV

If you're serious about living this new resurrection life with Christ, *act* like it. Pursue the things over which Christ presides. Don't shuffle along, eyes to the ground, absorbed with the things right in front of you. Look up, and be alert to what is going on around Christ—that's where the action is. See things from *his* perspective.

COLOSSIANS 3:1–2 MSG

We know that all things work together for good to those who love God, to those who are the called according to His purpose.

ROMANS 8:28 NKJV

Relationships

Two are better than one,
because they have a good return for their labor:
If either of them falls down,
one can help the other up.

ECCLESIASTES 4:9–10 NIV

Perfume and incense bring joy to the heart,
and the pleasantness of a friend springs
from their heartfelt advice.

PROVERBS 27:9 NIV

Love each other with genuine affection,
and take delight in honoring each other.

ROMANS 12:10 NLT

Above all else, guard your heart,
for everything you do flows from it.

PROVERBS 4:23 NIV

As those who have been chosen of God, holy
and beloved, put on a heart of compassion, kindness,
humility, gentleness and patience; bearing with
one another, and forgiving each other, whoever
has a complaint against anyone; just as the Lord
forgave you, so also should you. Beyond all these things
put on love, which is the perfect bond of unity.

COLOSSIANS 3:12–14 NASB

As iron sharpens iron,
so a friend sharpens a friend.

PROVERBS 27:17 NLT

Become complete. Be of good comfort,
be of one mind, live in peace; and the God of love and
peace will be with you.

2 CORINTHIANS 13:11 NKJV

Reliability

Every good and perfect gift is from above,
coming down from the Father of the heavenly lights,
who does not change like shifting shadows.

JAMES 1:17 NIV

You are near, LORD,
and all your commands are true.
Long ago I learned from your statutes
that you established them to last forever.

PSALM 119:151–152 NIV

The grass withers,
And its flower falls away,
But the word of the LORD endures forever.

1 PETER 1:24–25 NKJV

One who is faithful in a very little is also faithful in much.

Luke 16:10 esv

With all my heart I have sought You;
Do not let me wander from Your commandments.
Your word I have treasured in my heart,
That I may not sin against You.
Teach me, O Lord, the way of Your statutes,
And I shall observe it to the end.

Psalm 119:10–11, 33 nasb

Watch yourselves, so that you may not lose what we have
worked for, but may win a full reward.

2 John 1:8 esv

Respect

Do nothing out of selfish ambition or vain conceit.
Rather, in humility value others above yourselves,
not looking to your own interests but each of you
to the interests of the others.

PHILIPPIANS 2:3–4 NIV

For the Lord's sake, yield to the people who have
authority in this world.... It is God's desire that
by doing good you should stop foolish people from
saying stupid things about you. Live as free people,
but do not use your freedom as an excuse to do evil.
Live as servants of God. Show respect for all people:
Love the brothers and sisters of God's family.

1 PETER 2:13, 15–17 NCV

Have confidence in your leaders and submit
to their authority, because they keep watch over you as
those who must give an account. Do this so that
their work will be a joy, not a burden, for that
would be of no benefit to you.

HEBREWS 13:17 NIV

Appreciate those who diligently labor among you,
and have charge over you in the Lord and
give you instruction...esteem them very
highly in love because of their work.
Live in peace with one another.

1 THESSALONIANS 5:12–13 NASB

Serving

Each of you should use whatever gift you have received to serve others, as faithful stewards of God's grace in its various forms. If anyone serves, they should do so with the strength God provides, so that in all things God may be praised through Jesus Christ.

1 PETER 4:10–11 NIV

He who is greatest among you, let him be as the younger, and he who governs as he who serves. For who is greater, he who sits at the table, or he who serves? Is it not he who sits at the table? Yet I am among you as the One who serves.

LUKE 22:26–27 NKJV

Do you want to stand out? Then step down. Be a servant. If
you puff yourself up, you'll get the wind
knocked out of you. But if you're content to simply
be yourself, your life will count for plenty.

MATTHEW 23:11–12 MSG

Even the Son of Man did not come to be served, but to
serve, and to give His life a ransom for many.

MARK 10:45 NASB

You have been called to live in freedom,
my brothers and sisters. But don't use your freedom
to satisfy your sinful nature. Instead, use your freedom
to serve one another in love.

GALATIANS 5:13 NLT

Stress

Blessed is the one who trusts in the LORD,
whose confidence is in him.
They will be like a tree planted by the water
that sends out its roots by the stream.
It does not fear when heat comes;
its leaves are always green.
It has no worries in a year of drought
and never fails to bear fruit.

JEREMIAH 17:7–8 NIV

Give your entire attention to what God is doing right now,
and don't get worked up about what may or may not
happen tomorrow. God will help you deal with whatever
hard things come up when the time comes.

MATTHEW 6:34 MSG

Commit your actions to the Lord,
and your plans will succeed.

PROVERBS 16:3 NLT

The Lord also will be a refuge...in times of trouble.
Those who know Your name will put their trust in You;
For You, Lord, have not forsaken those who seek You.

PSALM 9:9–10 NKJV

May the God who gives endurance and encouragement
give you the same attitude of mind toward each other that
Christ Jesus had.

ROMANS 15:5 NIV

Thankfulness

Enter his gates with thanksgiving,
and his courts with praise!
Give thanks to him; bless his name!
For the LORD is good;
his steadfast love endures forever,
and his faithfulness to all generations.

PSALM 100:4–5 ESV

Rejoice always, pray without ceasing,
in everything give thanks; for this is the will of God.

1 THESSALONIANS 5:16–18 NKJV

Give thanks to the LORD, for he is good;
his love endures forever.

1 CHRONICLES 16:34 NIV

Let us come into his presence with thanksgiving;
let us make a joyful noise to him with songs of praise!

PSALM 95:2 ESV

Let us continually offer up a sacrifice of praise to God,
that is, the fruit of lips that give thanks to His name.

HEBREWS 13:15 NASB

I have learned how to be content with whatever I have.

PHILIPPIANS 4:11 NLT

We give thanks to God always for you, making mention of
you in our prayers; constantly bearing in mind your work
of faith and labor of love and steadfastness of hope.

1 THESSALONIANS 1:2−3 NASB

Trust

The LORD is my strength and my shield;
my heart trusts in him, and he helps me.

PSALM 28:7 NIV

May your whole self—spirit, soul, and body—
be kept safe and without fault when
our Lord Jesus Christ comes. You can trust the One
who calls you to do that for you.

1 THESSALONIANS 5:23–24 NCV

The law of the LORD is perfect,
refreshing the soul.
The statutes of the LORD are trustworthy,
making wise the simple.

PSALM 19:7 NIV

Those who know Your name will put their trust in You;
For You, LORD, have not forsaken those who seek You.

PSALM 9:10 NKJV

God's way is perfect.
All the LORD's promises prove true.
He is a shield for all who look to him for protection.
For who is God except the LORD?
Who but our God is a solid rock?

PSALM 18:30–31 NLT

May the God of hope fill you with all joy and peace as you
trust in him, so that you may overflow with hope by the
power of the Holy Spirit.

ROMANS 15:13 NIV

Truth

Teach me your ways, O Lord,
that I may live according to your truth!
Grant me purity of heart,
so that I may honor you.

PSALM 86:11 NLT

When he, the Spirit of truth, comes,
he will guide you into all the truth.

JOHN 16:13 NIV

The very essence of your words is truth;
all your just regulations will stand forever.

PSALM 119:160 NLT

Jesus said, "If you hold to my teaching,
you are really my disciples. Then you will know the truth,
and the truth will set you free."

JOHN 8:31–32 NIV

You desire truth in the innermost being,
And in the hidden part You will make me know wisdom.

PSALM 51:6 NASB

Truthful words stand the test of time,
but lies are soon exposed.

PROVERBS 12:19 NLT

Let us not love with words or speech
but with actions and in truth.

1 JOHN 3:18 NIV

Now that you have purified yourselves by obeying the truth
so that you have sincere love for each other,
love one another deeply, from the heart.

1 PETER 1:22 NIV

Unity

How good and pleasant it is
when God's people live together in unity!

PSALM 133:1 NIV

Every day they continued to meet together in the temple
courts. They broke bread in their homes and ate together
with glad and sincere hearts, praising God and enjoying the
favor of all the people. And the Lord added to their number
daily those who were being saved.

ACTS 2:46–47 NIV

I appeal to you, brothers, by the name of our Lord
Jesus Christ, that all of you agree, and that there be no
divisions among you, but that you be united in the
same mind and the same judgment.

1 CORINTHIANS 1:10 ESV

Holy Father...protect them by the power of your name
so that they will be united just as we are...that they
will all be one, just as you and I are one....
May they experience such perfect unity that
the world will know that you sent me and
that you love them as much as you love me.

JOHN 17:11, 21–23 NLT

Walk in a manner worthy of the calling to which
you have been called...bearing with one another in love,
eager to maintain the unity of the Spirit
in the bond of peace.

EPHESIANS 4:1–3 ESV

Wisdom

The wisdom from above is first of all pure.
It is also peace loving, gentle at all times, and willing to
yield to others. It is full of mercy and good deeds. It shows
no favoritism and is always sincere.

JAMES 3:17 NLT

Oh, the depth of the riches both of the wisdom
and knowledge of God! How unsearchable are His
judgments and unfathomable His ways!

ROMANS 11:33 NASB

Do not let wisdom and understanding out of your sight,
preserve sound judgment and discretion;
they will be life for you.

PROVERBS 3:21–22 NIV

Blessed are those who find wisdom,
those who gain understanding,
for she is more profitable than silver
and yields better returns than gold.
She is more precious than rubies;
nothing you desire can compare with her.
Long life is in her right hand;
in her left hand are riches and honor.
Her ways are pleasant ways,
and all her paths are peace.

PROVERBS 3:13–17 NIV

If any of you lacks wisdom, you should ask God,
who gives generously to all without finding fault,
and it will be given to you.

JAMES 1:5 NIV

Worry

Don't worry about anything; instead, pray about everything. Tell God what you need, and thank him for all he has done. Then you will experience God's peace, which exceeds anything we can understand. His peace will guard your hearts and minds as you live in Christ Jesus.

PHILIPPIANS 4:6–7 NLT

Which of you by worrying can add
a single hour to his life's span?

LUKE 12:25 NASB

Worry weighs a person down;
an encouraging word cheers a person up.

PROVERBS 12:25 NLT

Give your burdens to the Lord,
and he will take care of you.

PSALM 55:22 NLT

Do not worry about your life, what you will eat or drink;
or about your body, what you will wear. Is not life more
than food, and the body more than clothes?
Look at the birds of the air; they do not sow or reap or
store away in barns, and yet your heavenly Father
feeds them. Are you not much more valuable than they?

MATTHEW 6:25–26 NIV

May the Lord of peace himself give you peace
at all times in every way.

2 THESSALONIANS 3:16 ESV

Omega

Everyone who drinks this water will be thirsty again, but
whoever drinks the water I give them will never thirst.
Indeed, the water I give them will become in them a spring
of water welling up to eternal life.

JOHN 4:13–14 NIV

I am the Alpha and the Omega—the Beginning
and the End. To all who are thirsty I will give freely
from the springs of the water of life.

REVELATION 21:6 NLT

May the God of peace, who through
the blood of the eternal covenant brought back
from the dead our Lord Jesus, that great Shepherd
of the sheep, equip you with everything good
for doing his will, and may he work in us
what is pleasing to him, through Jesus Christ,
to whom be glory for ever and ever.
Amen.

HEBREWS 13:20-21 NIV